LEONARD COHEN
FOR UKULELE

Cover photo © Getty Images/Ann Johansson

ISBN: 978-1-5400-2232-5

Visit Hal Leonard Online at
www.halleonard.com

Contact Us:
Hal Leonard
7777 West Bluemound Road
Milwaukee, WI 53213
Email: info@halleonard.com

In Europe contact:
Hal Leonard Europe Limited
Distribution Centre, Newmarket Road
Bury St Edmunds, Suffolk, IP33 3YB
Email: info@halleonardeurope.com

In Australia contact:
Hal Leonard Australia Pty. Ltd.
4 Lentara Court
Cheltenham, Victoria, 3192 Australia
Email: info@halleonard.com.au

Anthem

Words and Music by Leonard Cohen

First note

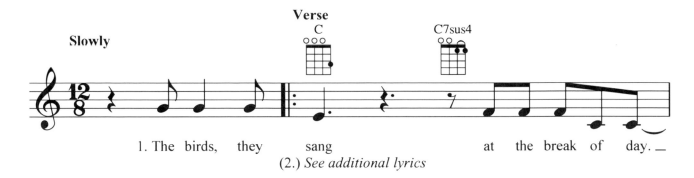

1. The birds, they sang at the break of day. __
(2.) *See additional lyrics*

__ "Start a - gain," __ I heard them

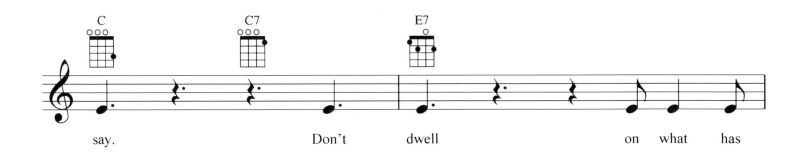

say. Don't dwell on what has

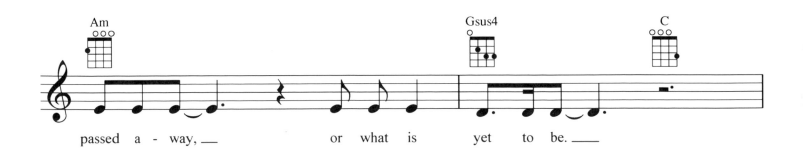

passed a - way, __ or what is yet to be. __

Yeah, the wars, ___ they will be

fought a - gain. ___ The ho - ly dove, she will ___ be

caught a - gain. ___ Bought and sold ___ and

bought a - gain, ___ the dove is nev - er free.

Chorus

Ring the bells that still can

ring. For - get your per - fect ___ of - fer -

3

love will come, but like a ref - u - gee. ___ (Ring,

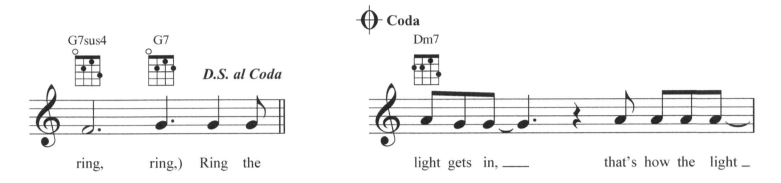

D.S. al Coda

ring, ring,) Ring the

Coda

light gets in, ___ that's how the light _

___ gets in, ___ that's how the light ___ gets in. ___

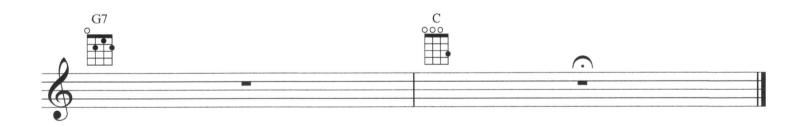

Additional Lyrics

2. We asked for signs, the signs were sent,
   The birth betrayed, the marriage spent.
   Yeah, the widowhood of every government,
   Signs for all to see.
   I can't run no more with that lawless crowd
   While the killers in high places say their prayers out loud.
   But they've summoned up a thundercloud,
   They're going to hear from me.

Bird on the Wire
(Bird on a Wire)

Words and Music by Leonard Cohen

If I, if I have been un - true, _____

I hope you know it was nev - er to you. 3. More like a

Verse

ba - by still - born, like a beast with his horn, I have

torn ev - 'ry - one _____ who reached out for me.

But I swear by this song, and by all _____ that I have done

wrong, I will make it all up to thee.

Bridge

I saw a beg-gar lean-ing on his wood-en crutch.

He said to me, "You must not ask for so much."

And a pret-ty wom-an lean-ing in her dark-ened door,

she cried to me, "Hey, why not ask for more?"

Outro-Verse

More like a bird on the wi-re, like a drunk in a mid-night choir, I have tried in my way to be free.

Chelsea Hotel #2

Words and Music by Leonard Cohen

I don't need you." And all of that jiv - ing a -

round. 2. I re -

Outro-Verse

3. I don't mean to sug - gest that I loved you the

best. I can't keep track of each fall - en rob - in.

I re - mem - ber you well in the Chel - sea Ho -

tel. That's all; I don't think of you that of - ten.

Everybody Knows

Words and Music by Leonard Cohen and Sharon Robinsoon

knows.

2. Ev - 'ry - bod - y knows that the boat is
5. *See additional lyrics*

leak - ing. Ev - 'ry - bod - y knows the cap - tain lied. Ev - 'ry - bod - y

got this bro - ken feel - ing, like their fa - ther or their dog just died. ___

___ Ev - 'ry - bod - y talk - ing to their pock - ets. Ev - 'ry - bod - y

wants a box of choc -'lates and a long - stem rose.

Ev - 'ry - bod - y knows.

3. Ev - 'ry - bod - y
6. *See additional lyrics*

Verse

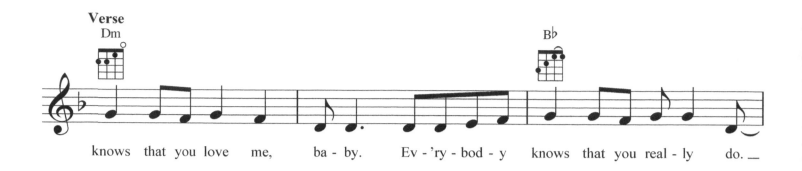

knows that you love me, ba - by. Ev - 'ry - bod - y knows that you real - ly do. __

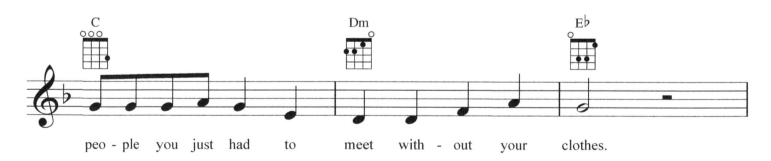

__ Ev - 'ry - bod - y knows that you've been faith - ful,

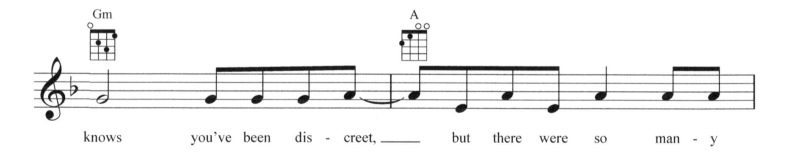

give or take a night or two. Ev - 'ry - bod - y

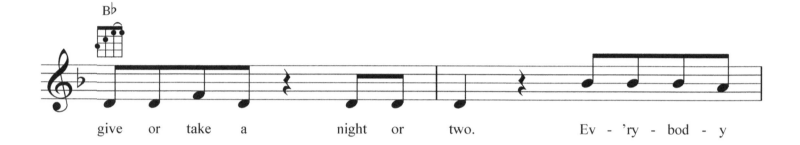

knows you've been dis - creet, _____ but there were so man - y

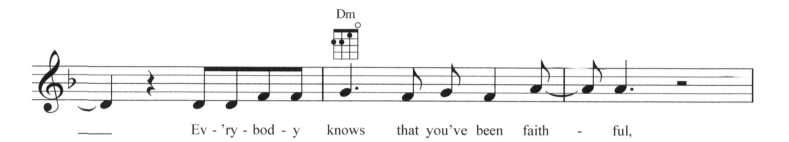

peo - ple you just had to meet with - out your clothes.

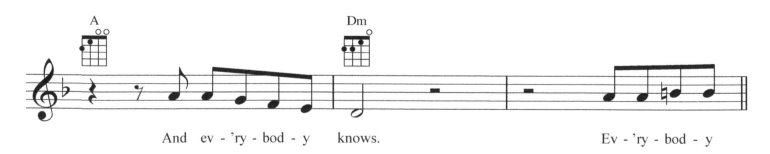

And ev - 'ry - bod - y knows. Ev - 'ry - bod - y

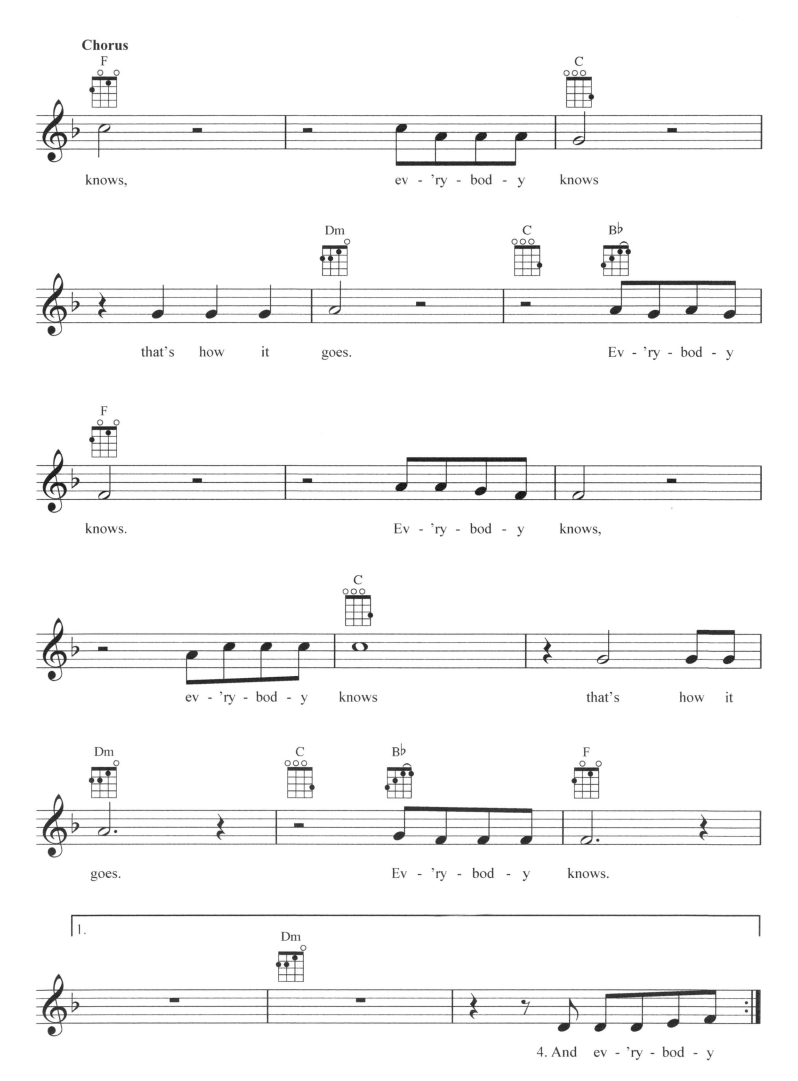

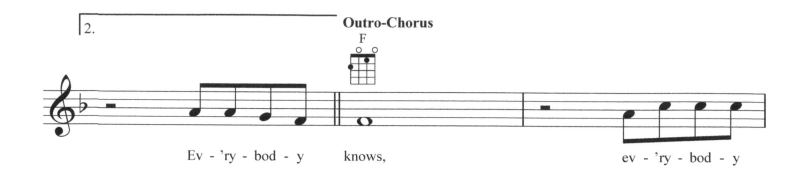

Outro-Chorus

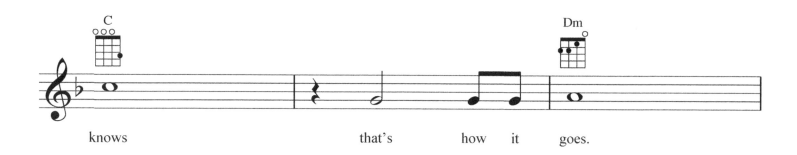

Ev - 'ry - bod - y   knows,   ev - 'ry - bod - y

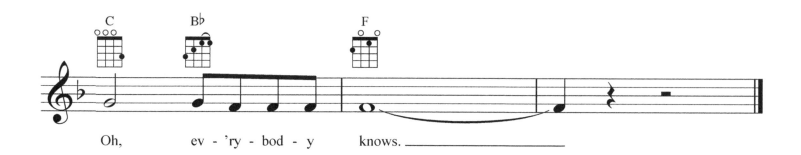

knows   that's   how   it   goes.

Oh,   ev - 'ry - bod - y   knows. _____

Additional Lyrics

4. And everybody knows that it's now or never.
   Everybody knows that it's me or you.
   And everybody knows that you live forever
   When you've done a line or two.
   Everybody knows the deal is rotten.
   Old Black Joe's still pickin' cotton
   For your ribbons and bows. And everybody knows.

5. Everybody knows that the plague is coming,
   Everybody knows that it's moving fast.
   Everybody knows that the naked man and woman
   Are just a shining artifact of the past.
   Everybody knows the scene is dead,
   But there's gonna be a meter on your bed
   That will disclose what everybody knows.

6. And everybody knows that you're in trouble.
   Everybody knows what you've been through,
   From the bloody cross on top of Calvary
   To the beach of Malibu.
   Everybody knows it's coming apart.
   Take one last look at this Sacred Heart
   Before it blows. And everybody knows.

Dance Me to the End of Love

Words and Music by Leonard Cohen

To Coda ⊕

dance me ____ to the end of love.

Yeah, dance ____ me to the end ____ of love. ____

Bridge

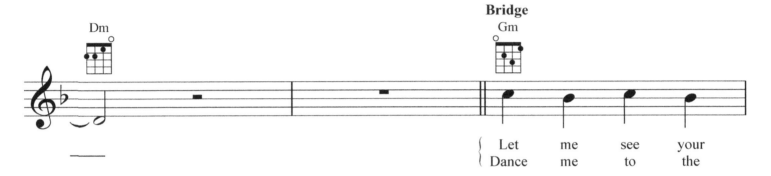

____ { Let me see your
Dance me to the

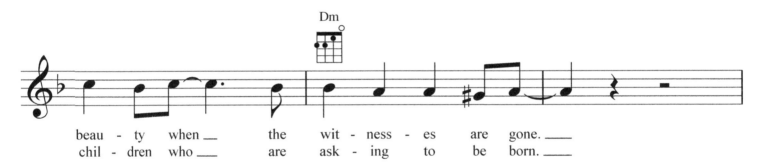

beau - ty when ____ the wit - ness - es are gone. ____
chil - dren who ____ are ask - ing to be born. ____

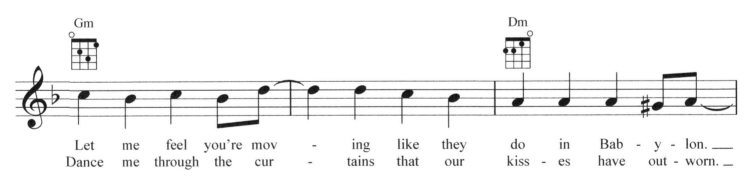

Let me feel you're mov - ing like they do in Bab - y - lon. ____
Dance me through the cur - tains that our kiss - es have out - worn. ____

____ Show me slow - ly what I on - ly know ____
____ Raise a tent of shel - ter now, ____ though ev -

Famous Blue Raincoat

Words and Music by Leonard Cohen

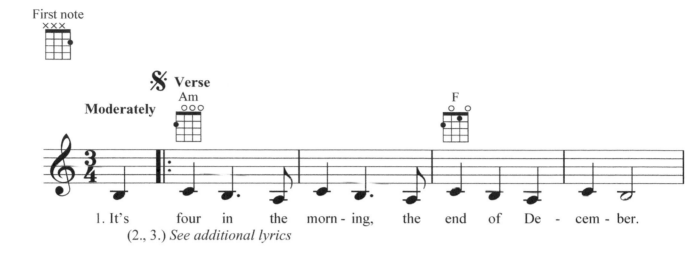

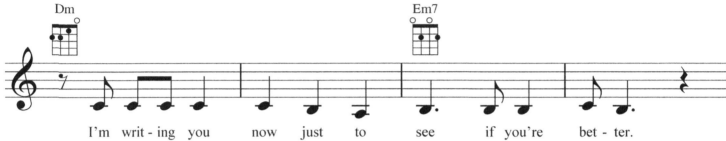

1. It's four in the morn - ing, the end of De - cem - ber.
(2., 3.) See additional lyrics

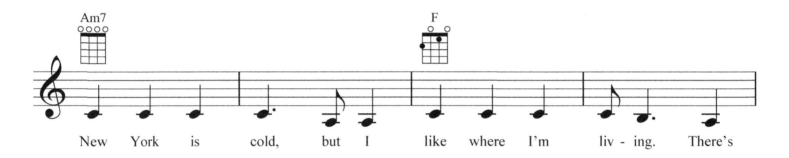

I'm writ - ing you now just to see if you're bet - ter.

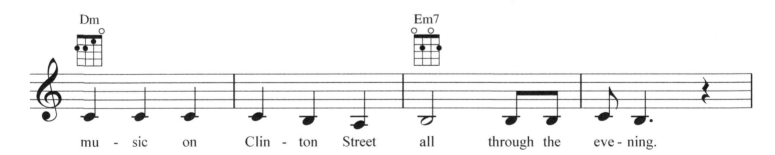

New York is cold, but I like where I'm liv - ing. There's

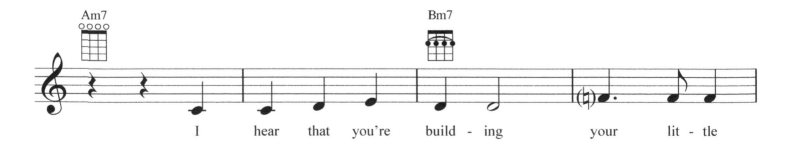

mu - sic on Clin - ton Street all through the eve - ning.

I hear that you're build - ing your lit - tle

house   deep   in   the   des - ert.

You're   liv - ing   for   noth - ing   now;   I   hope   you're

keep - ing   some   kind   of   rec - ord.   Yes, _____ and

Chorus

Jane   came   by   with   a   lock   of   your

hair.   She   said   that   you   gave   it   to

her   that   night   that   you   planned   to   go

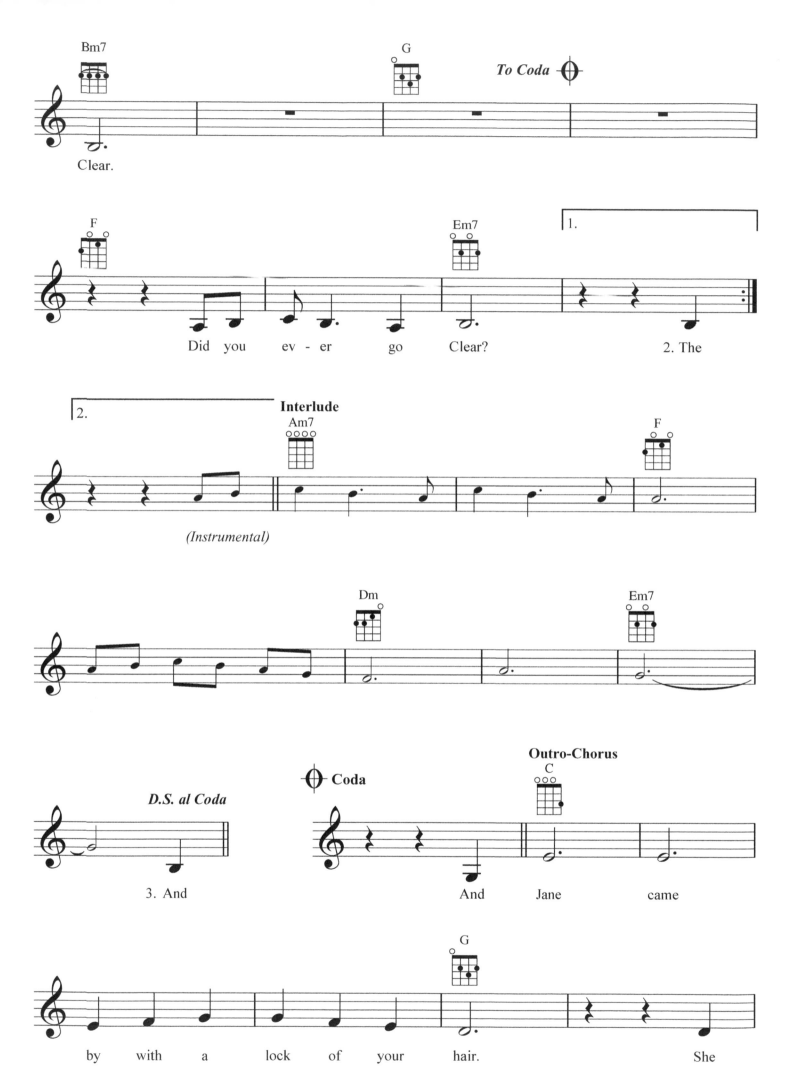

said that you gave it to her

that

night that you planned to go Clear.

Sin - cere - ly, L.

Co - hen.

Additional Lyrics

2. The last time we saw you, you looked so much older.
   Your famous blue raincoat was torn at the shoulder.
   You'd been to the station to meet every train,
   And you came home without Lili Marlene.
   And you treated my woman to a flake of your life,
   And when she came back, she was nobody's wife.

Chorus: Well, I see you there with a rose in your teeth, one more thin gypsy thief.
   Well, I see Jane's away; she sends her regards.

3. And what can I tell you, my brother, my killer?
   What can I possibly say?
   I guess that I miss you, I guess I forgive you.
   I'm glad you stood in my way.
   If you ever come by here for Jane or for me,
   Well, your enemy is sleeping and his woman is free.

Chorus: Yes, thanks for the trouble you took from her eyes.
   I thought it was there for good, so I never tried.

First We Take Manhattan

Words and Music by Leonard Cohen

First note

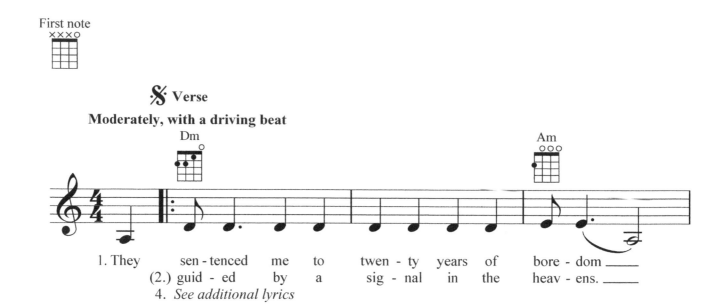

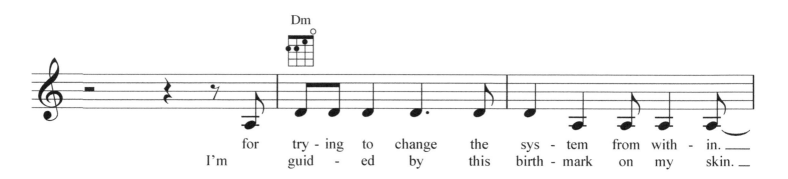

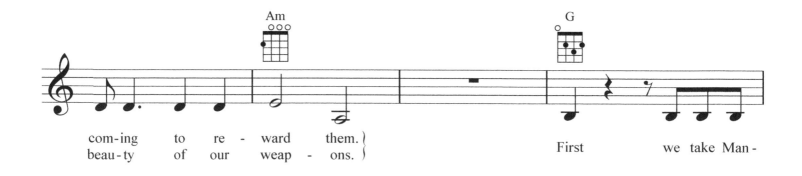

hat - tan,   then we take Ber - lin. _____

1.   2., 3.

2. I'm   I'd

Bridge

real - ly like to live be - side ___ you, ba - by. ___

I love your bod - y   and your spir - it   and your

clothes.   But you see that line there

mov - ing through the sta - tion? _____   And I

First we take Man - hat - tan,

To Coda ⊕

then we take Ber - lin. _____

D.S. al Coda
(take 2nd ending)

⊕ **Coda**

lin.

6. Ah, re -

Outro-Verse

mem - ber me; ___ I used to live for mu - sic.

And re - mem - ber me; I brought your gro - c'ries

in.   Well, it's   Fa - ther's   Day ___

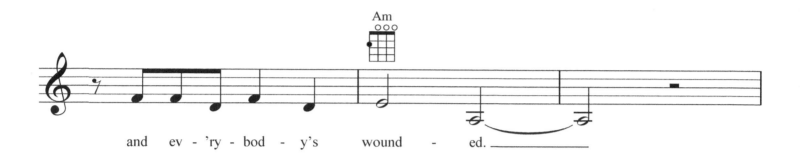

and ev - 'ry - bod - y's   wound - ed. _____

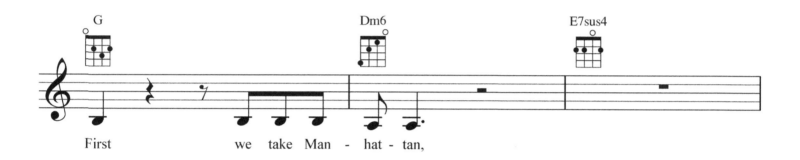

First   we take Man - hat - tan,

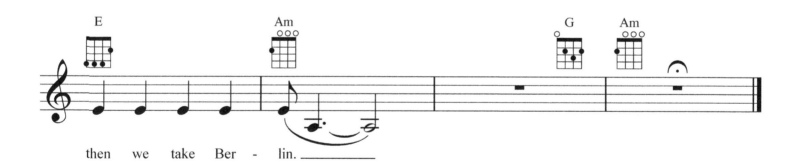

then we take Ber - lin. _____

Additional Lyrics

4. I don't like your fashion business, mister.
   I don't like these drugs that keep you thin.
   I don't like what happened to my sister,
   First we take Manhattan, then we take Berlin.

5. And I thank you for those items that you sent me:
   The monkey and the plywood violin.
   I practiced every night and now I'm ready.
   First we take Manhattan, then we take Berlin.

Hallelujah

Words and Music by Leonard Cohen

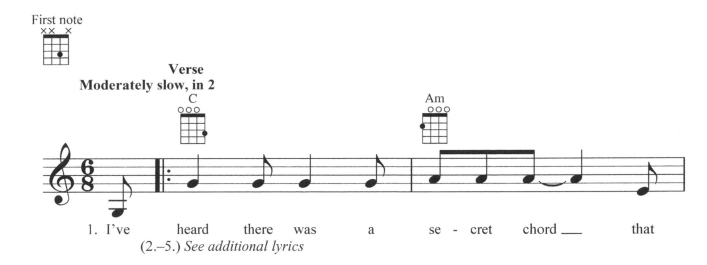

1. I've heard there was a se-cret chord ___ that
(2.–5.) *See additional lyrics*

Da-vid played ___ and it pleased the Lord, ___ but you don't ___ real-ly

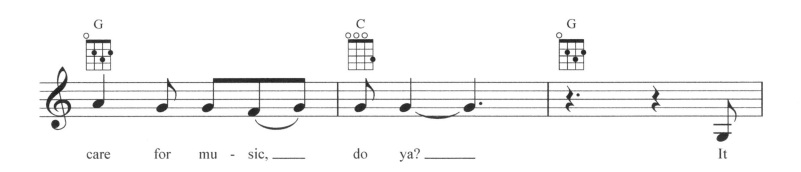

care for mu-sic, ___ do ya? ___ It

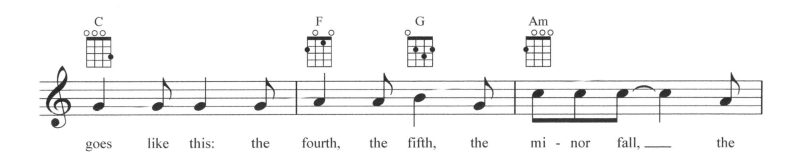

goes like this: the fourth, the fifth, the mi-nor fall, ___ the

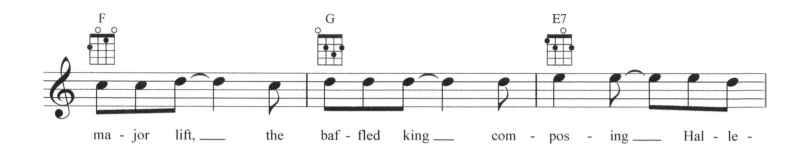

ma - jor lift, ___ the baf - fled king ___ com - pos - ing ___ Hal - le -

Chorus

lu - jah. _____ Hal - le - lu - jah, _____ hal - le -

lu - jah, _____ hal - le - lu - jah, _____ hal - le -

1.–4.

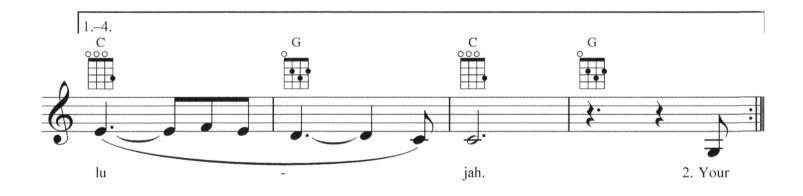

lu - jah. 2. Your

5.

Outro-Chorus

lu - jah. Hal - le - lu - jah. _____ Hal - le -

lu - jah. _____ Hal - le - lu - jah. _____ Hal - le -

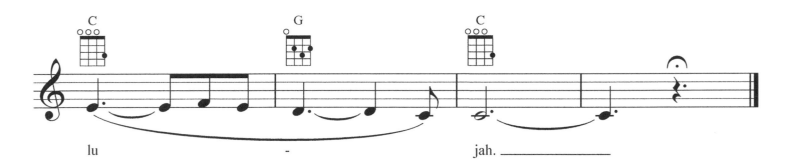

lu - jah. _____

Additional Lyrics

2. Your faith was strong but you needed proof.
   You saw her bathing on the roof.
   Her beauty and the moonlight overthrew ya.
   She tied you to a kitchen chair.
   She broke your throne, she cut your hair.
   And from your lips she drew the Hallelujah.

3. Maybe I have been here before.
   I know this room, I've walked this floor.
   I used to live alone before I knew ya.
   I've seen your flag on the marble arch.
   Love is not a vict'ry march.
   It's a cold and it's a broken Hallelujah.

4. There was a time you let me know
   What's real and going on below.
   But now you never show it to me, do ya?
   And remember when I moved in you.
   The holy dark was movin', too,
   And every breath we drew was Hallelujah.

5. Maybe there's a God above,
   And all I ever learned from love
   Was how to shoot at someone who outdrew ya.
   And it's not a cry you can hear at night.
   It's not somebody who's seen the light.
   It's a cold and it's a broken Hallelujah.

The Future

Words and Music by Leonard Cohen

First note

Verse
Moderately bright

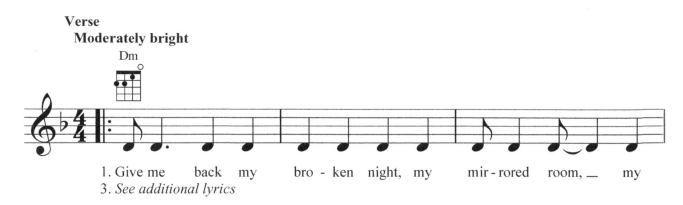

1. Give me back my bro-ken night, my mir-rored room, — my
3. *See additional lyrics*

se - cret life. __ It's lone - ly here; there's no one left to tor -

- ture. Give me ab - so - lute con - trol

o - ver ev - 'ry liv - ing soul, and lie be - side __ me, ba - by.

rec - tions; won't be noth - ing, noth - ing you can

meas - ure an - y - more. ____ The bliz - zard, the

bliz - zard of the world has crossed the thresh - old and it's o - ver - turned the

or - der of the soul. When they said, "Re - pent, __

____ re - pent," __ I won - der what they meant. __

When they said, ____ "Re - pent, ____ re - pent," __

I won - der what they meant. ___ When they

said, "Re - pent, ___ re - pent," ___ I won - der

what they meant. ___

Bridge

There'll be the break - ing of the an - cient West - ern ___ code.

Your pri - vate life will sud - den - ly ex - plode. ___

There'll be phan - toms, there'll be fires ___ on the road,

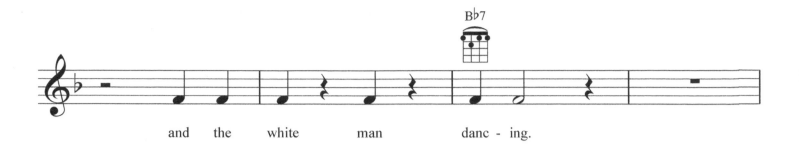

and the white man danc - ing.

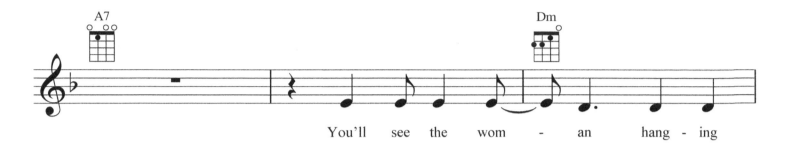

You'll see the wom - an hang - ing

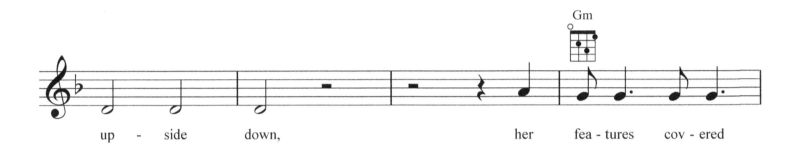

up - side down, her fea - tures cov - ered

by her fall - en gown, ___ and all the

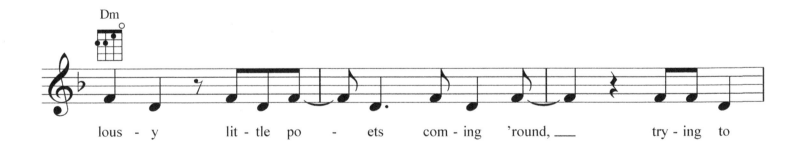

lous - y lit - tle po - ets com - ing 'round, ___ try - ing to

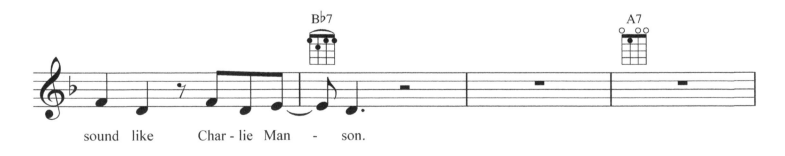

sound like Char - lie Man - son.

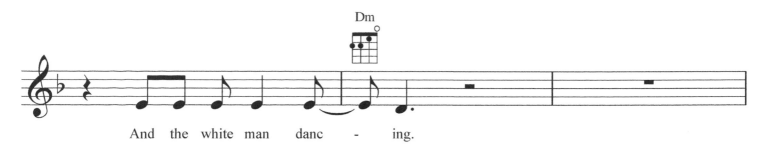

And the white man danc - ing.

D.S. al Coda

Coda

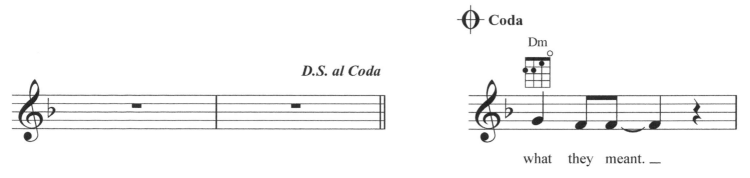

what they meant. —

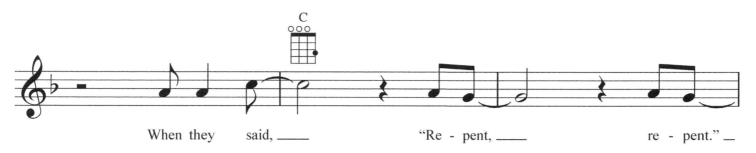

When they said, _____ "Re - pent, _____ re - pent." —

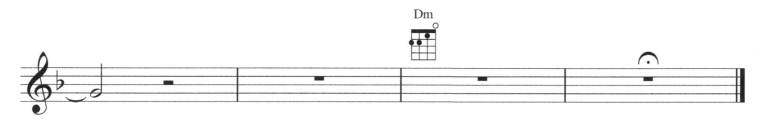

—

Additional Lyrics

3. You don't know me from the wind.
   You never will, you never did.
   I'm the little Jew who wrote the Bible.
   I've seen the nations rise and fall,
   I've heard their stories, heard them all,
   But love's the only engine of survival.
   Your servant here, he has been told
   To say it clear, to say it cold:
   It's over, it ain't goin' any further.
   But now the wheels of heaven stop,
   You feel the devil's ridin' crop.
   Get ready for the future; it is murder.

4. Give me back the Berlin Wall,
   Give me Stalin and St. Paul,
   Give me Christ or give me Hiroshima.
   Destroy another fetus now;
   We don't like children anyhow.
   I've seen the future, baby; it is murder.

Hey, That's No Way to Say Goodbye

Words and Music by Leonard Cohen

First note

Verse
Moderately slow, flowing

1. I loved you in the morn - ing, our kiss - es deep and warm, ___ your
(2., 3.) *See additional lyrics*

hair up - on the pil - low like a sleep - y gold - en storm. ___ Yes, ___

___ man - y loved be - fore ___ us, I know that we are not new. ___ In

cit - y and in for - est, they smiled like me and you. ___ But

now it's come to dis - tanc - es and both of us must try. ___ Your

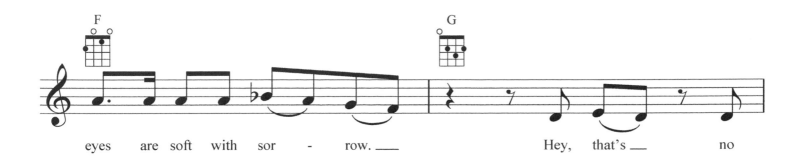

eyes   are soft with sor - row. ____   Hey, that's __   no

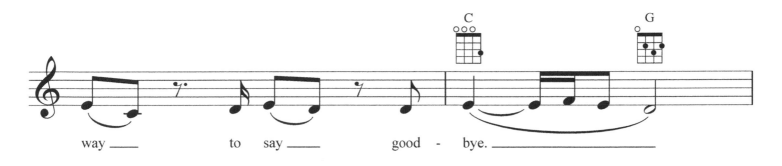

way __   to say __   good - bye. _____

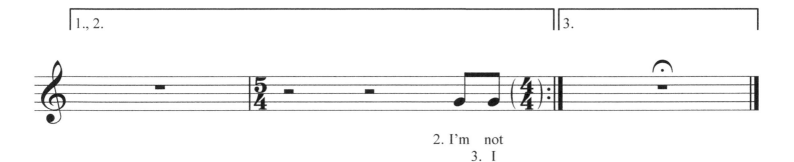

1., 2.   3.

2. I'm not
3. I

Additional Lyrics

2. I'm not looking for another
   As I wander in my time.
   Walk me to the corner;
   Our steps will always rhyme.
   You know my love goes with you
   As your love stays with me.
   It's just the way it changes
   Like the shoreline and the sea.
   But let's not talk of love or chains
   And things we can't untie.
   Your eyes are soft with sorrow.
   Hey, that's no way to say goodbye.

3. I loved you in the morning,
   Our kisses deep and warm,
   Your hair upon the pillow
   Like a sleepy golden storm.
   Yes, many loved before us;
   I know that we are not new.
   In city and in forest,
   They smiled like me and you.
   But let's not talk of love or chains
   And things we can't untie.
   Your eyes are soft with sorrow.
   Hey, that's no way to say goodbye.

I'm Your Man

Words and Music by Leonard Cohen

beast won't go to sleep. ___ I've been run-ning through these

prom-is-es to you that I made and I could not keep. ___ Ah, but a

man nev-er got a wom-an back, ___ not by beg-ging on his knees. ___

___ Or I'd crawl to you, ba-by, and I'd fall at your feet, ___ and I'd

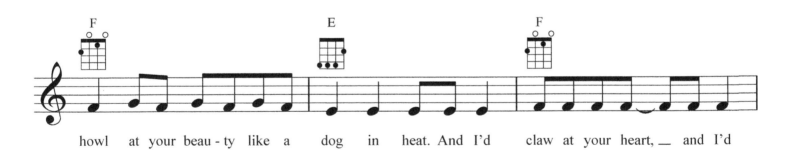

howl at your beau-ty like a dog in heat. And I'd claw at your heart, ___ and I'd

tear at your sheet. I'd say, "Please, ___ please, ___ I'm your

man." _

3. And if you've got to sleep for a mo - ment

on the road, _ I will steer for you. _ And if you want to

work the street a - lone, ____ I'll dis - ap - pear for you.

If you want a fa - ther ____ for your child, ____ or on - ly want to

walk with me a while a - cross the sand, _

I'm your man. _

So Long Marianne

Words and Music by Leonard Cohen

First note

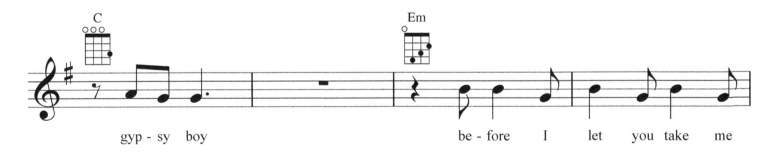

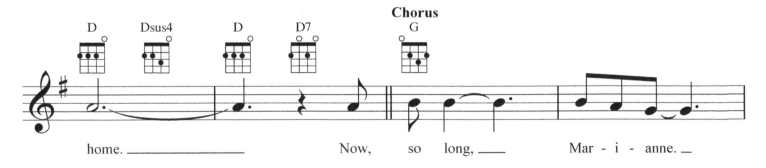

It's time that we be-gan ___ to laugh and cry and

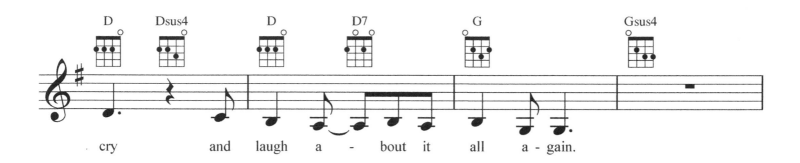

cry and laugh a - bout it all a - gain.

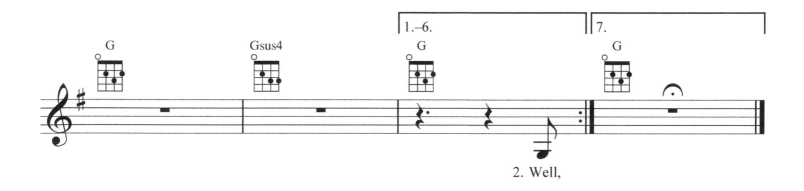

2. Well,

Additional Lyrics

2. Well, you know that I love to live with you,
   But you make me forget so very much.
   I forget to pray for the angel,
   And then the angels forget to pray for us.

3. We met when we were almost young,
   Deep in the green lilac park.
   You held on to me like I was a crucifix
   As we went kneeling through the dark.

4. Your letters, they all say that you're beside me now.
   Then why do I feel alone?
   I'm standing on a ledge, and your fine spider web
   Is fastening my ankle to a stone.

5. For now I need your hidden love;
   I'm cold as a new razor blade.
   You left when I told you I was curious;
   I never said that I was brave.

6. Oh, you're really such a pretty one.
   I see you've gone and changed your name again,
   And just when I climbed this whole mountainside
   To wash my eyelids in the rain.

7. Oh, your eyes, well, I forget your eyes.
   Your body's at home in every sea.
   How come you gave away your news to everyone
   That you said was a secret for me?

A Thousand Kisses Deep

Words and Music by Leonard Cohen and Sharon Robinson

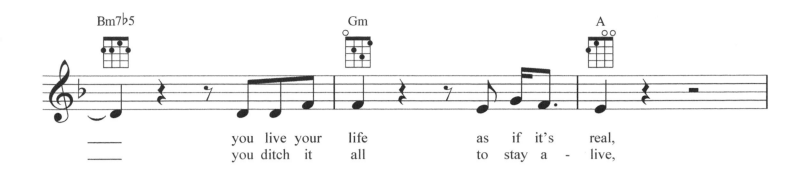

Bm7♭5   Gm   A

____ you live your life   as   if   it's   real,
____ you ditch it   all   to   stay   a -   live,

B♭   C   1.   Dm   2.   Dm

a thou - sand kiss - es   deep. _____   2. I'm turn - ing
a thou - sand kiss - es   deep. __   ____   *(Instrumental)*

𝄋 Interlude

Dm   A   Dm

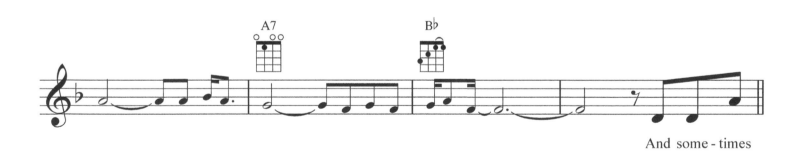

A7   B♭

And some - times

Bridge

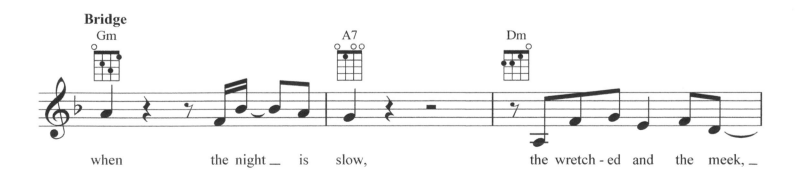

Gm   A7   Dm

when   the night __ is   slow,   the wretch - ed   and   the   meek, __

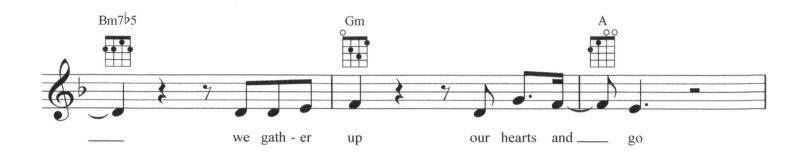

we gath - er up   our hearts and ___ go

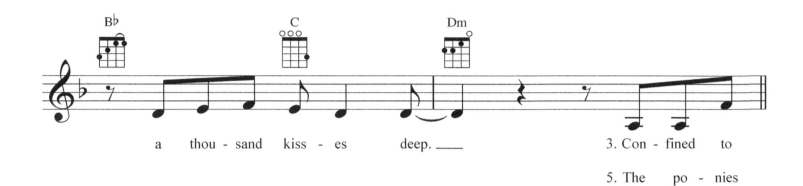

a   thou - sand   kiss - es   deep. ___   3. Con - fined   to

5. The   po - nies

Verse

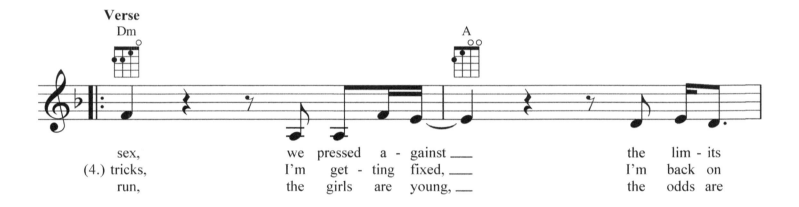

sex,   we   pressed a - gainst ___   the   lim - its
(4.) tricks,   I'm   get - ting fixed, ___   I'm   back on
run,   the   girls are young, ___   the   odds are

of the sea. ___   I   saw there were   no   o - ceans ___
Boo - gie Street. ___   I   guess they won't   ex - change the ___
there to beat. ___   You   win   a   while   and then it's ___

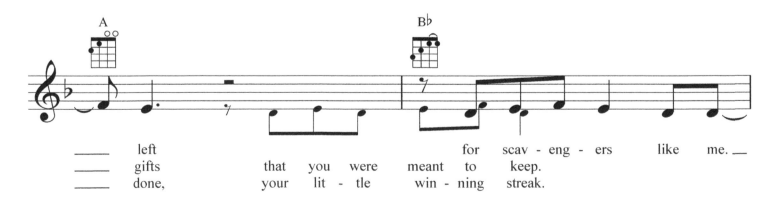

___ left   for scav - eng - ers like me. ___
___ gifts   that you were meant to   keep.
___ done,   your lit - tle win - ning streak.

I made it to the for - ward
And qui - et is the thought _ of
And sum - moned now to deal _

deck, I blessed our rem - nant _ fleet, _ and then con -
you, the file on you com - plete, _ ex - cept what
_ with your in - vin - ci - ble de - feat, _ you live your

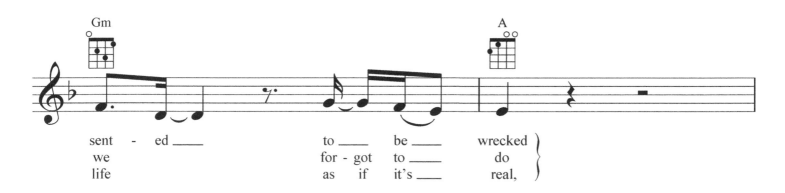

sent - ed _ to _ be _ wrecked
we for - got to _ do
life as if it's _ real,

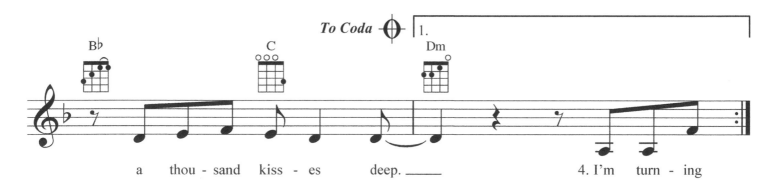

a thou - sand kiss - es deep. _____ 4. I'm turn - ing

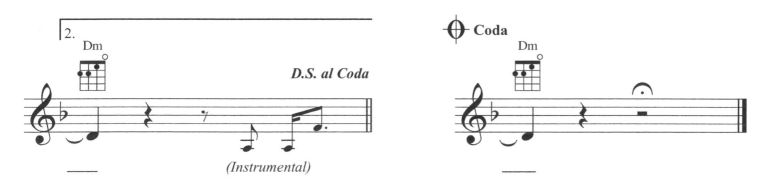

(Instrumental) _____

Waiting for the Miracle

Words and Music by Leonard Cohen and Sharon Robinson

do   when you're beg - ging for a crumb. ___ Noth - in' left to

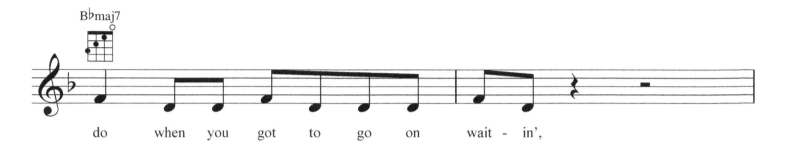

do   when you got to go on wait - in',

wait - in' ___ for the mir - a - cle ___ to come.

D.C. al Coda 1
(with repeat)

4. Now I

Coda 1

Noth - in' left to

Chorus

do   when you know ___ you've been tak - en, noth - in' left to

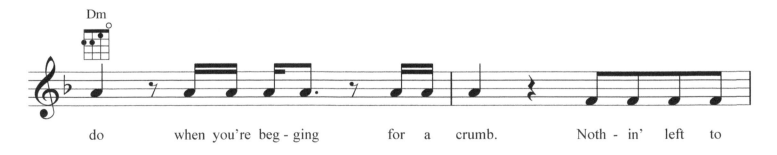

do   when you're beg - ging for a crumb. Noth - in' left to

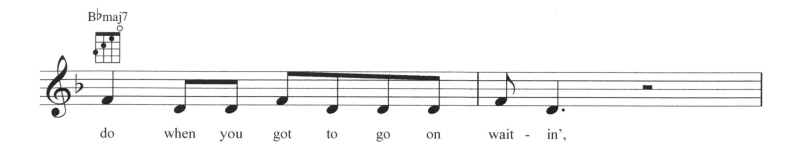

do when you got to go on wait - in',

wait - in' for the mir - a - cle to come.

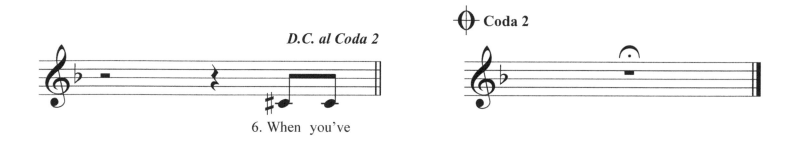

D.C. al Coda 2

⊕ **Coda 2**

6. When you've

Additional Lyrics

2. I know you really loved me,
   But, you see, my hands were tied.
   And I know it must have hurt you,
   It must have hurt your pride
   To have to stand beneath my window
   With your bugle and your drum.
   And me, I'm up there waitin'
   For the miracle, for the miracle to come.

3. I don't believe you'd like it,
   You wouldn't like it here.
   There ain't no entertainment
   And the judgements are severe.
   The Maestro says it's Mozart,
   But it sounds like bubble gum
   When you're waitin'
   For the miracle, for the miracle to come.

4. Now I dreamed about you, baby;
   It was just the other night.
   Most of you was naked,
   Ah, but some of you was light.
   The sands of time were fallin'
   From your fingers and your thumb,
   And you were waitin'
   For the miracle, for the miracle to come.

5. Now, baby, let's get married;
   We've been alone too long.
   Let's be alone together,
   Let's see if we're that strong.
   Yeah, let's do somethin' crazy,
   Somethin' absolutely wrong
   While we're waitin'
   For the miracle, for the miracle to come.

6. When you've fallen on the highway
   And you're lyin' in the rain,
   When they ask you how you're doin',
   Of course, you say you can't complain.
   If you're squeezed for information,
   That's when you've got to play it dumb.
   You just say you're out there waitin'
   For the miracle, for the miracle to come.

Suzanne

Words and Music by Leonard Cohen

First note

Verse
Moderately, flowing

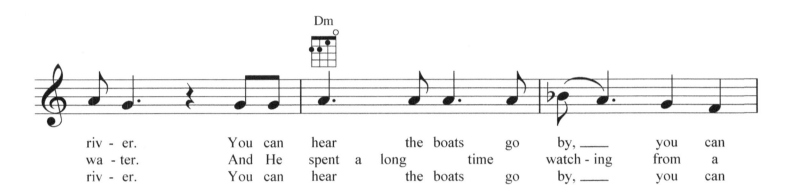

1. Su - zanne takes you down ___ to her place by the
(2.) Je - sus was a sail - or when He walked up - on the
(3.) zanne takes you down ___ to her place by the

riv - er. You can hear the boats go by, ___ you can
wa - ter. And He spent a long time watch - ing from a
riv - er. You can hear the boats go by, ___ you can

spend the night for - ev - er. _____ And you know that she's half
lone - ly wood - en tow - er. _____ And when He knew for
spend the night for - ev - er. _____ And the sun pours down like

cra - zy and that's why you want to be there; and she
cer - tain on - ly drown - ing men could see Him, He
hon - ey on our la - dy of the har - bour; and she

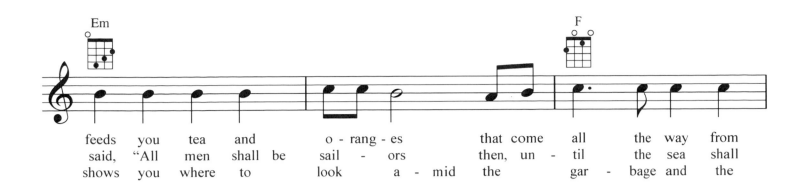

feeds you tea and o - rang - es that come all the way from
said, "All men shall be sail - ors then, un - til the sea shall
shows you where to look a - mid the gar - bage and the

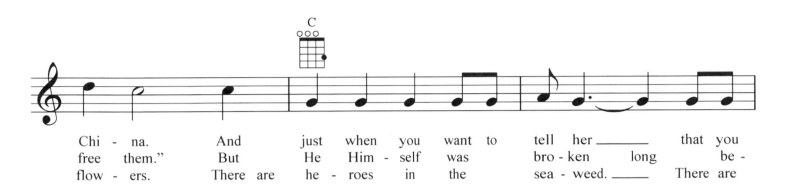

Chi - na. And just when you want to tell her _____ that you
free them." But He Him - self was bro - ken long be -
flow - ers. There are he - roes in the sea - weed. _____ There are

have no love to give her, _____ she gets you on her
fore the sky would o - pen. _____ For - sak - en, al - most
chil - dren in the morn - ing. _____ They are lean - ing out for

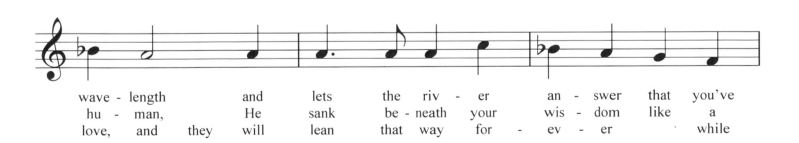

wave - length and lets the riv - er an - swer that you've
hu - man, He lets sank be - neath your wis - dom like a
love, and they will lean that way for - ev - er while

al - ways _____ been her lov - er. _____ And you
stone. _____ And you
Su - zanne _____ holds her mir - ror. _____ And you

want   to   trav - el   with   her, _____ and you   want   to   trav - el
want   to   trav - el   with   Him, _____ and you   want   to   trav - el
want   to   trav - el   with   her, _____ and you   want   to   trav - el

blind, _____ and you   think   you may - be   trust   her, _____ 'cause she's
blind, _____ and you   think   you may - be   trust   Him, _____ for He's
blind, _____ and you   think   may - be you'll trust   her, _____ for you've

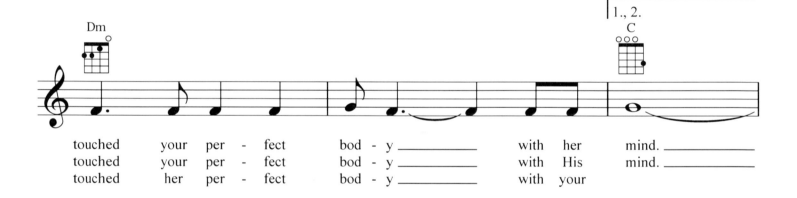

touched   your per - fect   bod - y _____ with   her   mind. _____
touched   your per - fect   bod - y _____ with   His   mind. _____
touched   her   per - fect   bod - y _____ with   your

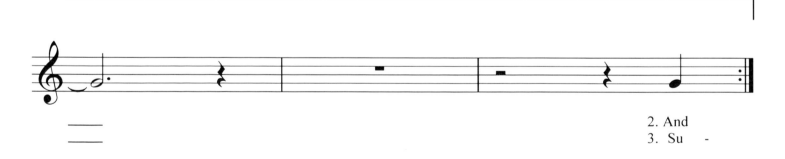

____
____

2. And
3. Su -

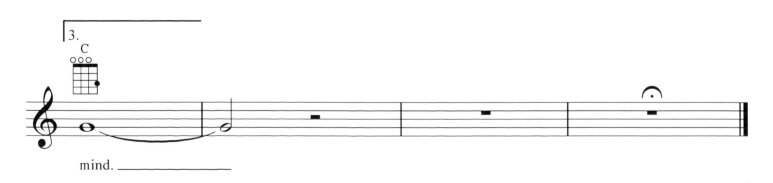

mind. _____